A 31-DAY DEVOTIONAL

Good Morning, My Love

LOVE LETTERS FROM JESUS, LOVER OF YOUR SOUL

Good Morning, My Love
ISBN: 978-0-578-64711-1
Copyright © 2020 by Because of Jesus Publishing
P.O. Box 3064
Broken Arrow, OK 74013-3064

Cover Design by: Nancy Bishop
nbishopsdesigns.com

Editing and Interior Design by: Yattira Editing Services
www.yattira.com

Table of Contents

Endorsement
By Nichole Marbach

Good Morning, My Love, by my friend Connie Witter, will bless all who read this powerful devotional book. I believe that as you read these daily love letters from Jesus, you will understand in a deeper way how much Jesus extravagantly loves and cherishes you.

This book will help you start your day by reminding you that you are passionately loved and treasured and as a result, truth will replace lies and freedom will be the result. Knowing we are deeply loved by God, I believe, is the key to healing and wholeness in every area of our lives. This beautiful devotional book will bring peace to your heart as you soak in these letters and the powerful scriptures that conclude each day.

I highly recommend this book for anyone who wants a deeper revelation of the love of Jesus. There is nothing greater than knowing we are passionately loved.

Nichole Marbach
Founder, Nichole Marbach Ministries

Personal Note from the Author

This devotional came out of a longing of my heart to know Jesus more fully and His great love for me. At this time in my life, I had already been radically transformed by a revelation of His amazing love for me, but I knew there was more of His love to be discovered. His unchanging, unfailing love is the only thing that has ever truly satisfied my soul. Several years ago as I was sharing my heart with Jesus, I prayed, *"Jesus, I know You love me, but I also know there is so much more of Your love to understand and discover. Open my eyes and help me to see the depths of Your endless love for me."*

Ephesians 3:17-20 came up in my heart, as I prayed, *"Jesus, take me deeper, higher, and wider into the depths of your extravagant love. I want every thought in my mind, every belief of my heart, and every cell of my body to be flooded with your love. I want to experience the fullness of your life in me."*

In answer to this heartfelt prayer, Jesus took me to the Song of Songs. It's a mysterious book of the Bible, full of symbolism and wonder, but I was about to have my eyes opened to a love so deep that I would never be the same. The Holy Spirit took me on a journey verse by verse into the heart of Jesus and His beautiful love song over me, His beloved bride. As I began to study this beautiful book of the Bible and ask Jesus to reveal His love to me, I began to hear Him speak into the depths of my soul, coming to the places where I was still hiding behind lies, bringing me out of darkness into His marvelous light.

As He spoke into the depths of my soul, I began to write down in my journal those beautiful words of love that He spoke to my heart. In this 31 day devotional, I share those love letters that Jesus is speaking not only to me, but to you, His beloved bride.

As you read each day's devotion, I encourage you to ask Jesus to reveal His great love for you personally. Are you ready to be radically transformed by a deeper revelation of Jesus' passionate, unchanging love for you? Are you ready to live as one with Jesus and truly reign in life as His beloved bride? Then I invite you on this 31 day journey into an incredible, extravagant love affair with Jesus! Your life will never be the same!

Ephesians 3:16-20 (TPT) is my prayer for you:

"16 I pray that he would unveil within you the unlimited riches of his glory and favor until supernatural strength floods your innermost being with his divine might and explosive power.

"17 Then, by constantly using your faith, the life of Christ will be released deep inside you, and the resting place of his love will become the very source and root of your life.

"18-19 Then you will be empowered to discover what every holy one experiences—the great magnitude of the astonishing love of Christ in all its dimensions. How deeply intimate and far-reaching is his love! How enduring and inclusive it is! Endless love beyond measurement that transcends our understanding—this extravagant love pours into you until you are filled to overflowing with the fullness of God!

"20 Never doubt God's mighty power to work in you and accomplish all this. He will achieve infinitely more than your greatest request, your most unbelievable dream, and exceed your wildest imagination! He will outdo them all, for his miraculous power constantly energizes you."

— Connie Witter

Prayer of Salvation

John 3:16-17:

"16 For this is how much God loved the world—he gave his one and only, unique Son as a gift. So now everyone who believes in him will never perish but experience everlasting life. 17 God did not send his Son into the world to judge and condemn the world, but to be its Savior and rescue it!" (TPT).

If you've never said, "Yes!" to Jesus, I invite you to receive His extravagant love for you today:

Heavenly Father, I believe that Jesus Christ died to take away all my sin and rose again to make me one with Him. Today I receive Your abundance of grace toward me and Your free gift of righteousness in Christ! Today I say, "Yes!" to Jesus and I receive Him as my Lord and Savior. Thank You for the gift of eternal life. I love You because You first loved me!

If you prayed this prayer and believed on Jesus, you became a brand-new creation in Christ Jesus. You became the bride of Christ! The Bible says the angels of heaven are rejoicing over you (Luke 15:10).

I would love to hear from you! Please contact me at www.conniewitter.com and let me know of your decision to make Jesus the Lord of your life.

Day 1
Let Me Love You

Good morning, My love,

Let Me smother you with kisses, My beloved bride, for you are My greatest delight. My words of affirmation are divine kisses upon your heart. I will remind you over and over again of how I see you, until you believe that what I say is true!

Look at you, My dearest darling: you are so lovely! You are beauty itself to Me! I chose you to be My beloved bride, and when you said, "Yes," to Me, we became one and My heart was filled with ecstatic delight! I am yours and you are Mine; to take care of you brings me great joy! As you trust my perfect love for you, it will drive all fear from your heart. There is absolutely nothing you could ever do to keep Me from loving you!

Will you let Me love you by believing what I say? Will you say, "Yes!" to My great love for you today? If you let My love define you, you will shine with My glory for the whole world to see. It's time, My love, to arise, and reign as one with Me!

– Your Bridegroom, Jesus

Song of Songs 1:1-2 *(TPT)*:

1 The most amazing song of all, by King Solomon. **The Shulamite** *2 Let him smother me with kisses—his Spirit-kiss divine. So kind are your caresses, I drink them in like the sweetest wine!*

Song of Songs 1:15 *(TPT)*:

The Shepherd-King *Look at you, my dearest darling, you are so lovely! You are beauty itself to me.*

1 John 4:15-16 *(NCV)*:

15 Whoever confesses that Jesus is the Son of God has God living inside, and that person lives in God. 16 And so we know the love that God has for us, and we trust that love.

1 John 4:17-18 *(AMPC)*:

17 In this [union and communion with Him] love is brought to completion and attains perfection with us, that we may have confidence for the day of judgment [with assurance and boldness to face Him], because as He is, so are we in this world. 18 There is no fear in love [dread does not exist], but full-grown (complete, perfect) love turns fear out of doors and expels every trace of terror! For fear brings with it the thought of punishment, and [so] he who is afraid has not reached the full maturity of love [is not yet grown into love's complete perfection].

Romans 8:39 *(NLT)*:

No power in the sky above or in the earth below— indeed, nothing in all creation will ever be able to separate us from the love of God that is revealed in Christ Jesus our Lord.

2 Corinthians 1:20 *(NCV)*:

The yes to all of God's promises is in Christ, and through Christ we say yes to the glory of God.

Take a moment to think about what Jesus said about you, and what He asked of you. Will you let Him love you by believing what He says? Will you say, "Yes!" to Him today? Write down how His words of love spoke to your heart.

"Let me take care of these things concerning you."

Dread → Joy!

Jesus, I'm ready to let You love me. When You look at me, beauty is what You see! Smother me with Your divine kisses, and transform me with Your love. I say, "Yes" to every word You speak over me. I receive Your love for me today.

– Your beloved Bride

Day 2
True Life is Found in Me

Good morning, My love,

I came to share My life with you! I want your heart to overflow with My joy, My peace, My approval, and My unconditional, unfailing love! Sometimes I see you feeling discouraged and dissatisfied with yourself and your life. Your heart feels sad when you look somewhere besides Me to define your life.

When you look to the world for approval, success, and validation, it will always lead to disappointment. All the world has to offer will never bring you true satisfaction in life. That place in your heart where you long for unconditional love, approval, acceptance, and worth was created to be filled with Me and My love for you! But every day you get to choose where you will go to satisfy these longings of your heart.

Oh, My beautiful one, how I long for you to choose Me! Long before I created the world, you were on My mind! I chose you as the focus of My love, to be made whole and holy by My love! Let My words of love define who you truly are! For My words are spirit and they are life! Drink the living water that I give to you; we will share My life together, and you will be completely satisfied!

— Your Bridegroom, Jesus

Song of Songs 1:4 *(TPT)*:

Draw me into your heart. We will run away together into the king's cloud-filled chamber. We will remember your love, rejoicing and delighting in you, celebrating your every kiss as better than wine. No wonder righteousness adores you!

Ephesians 1:4 *(MSG)*:

Long before he laid down earth's foundations, he had us in mind, had settled on us as the focus of his love, to be made whole and holy by his love.

Proverbs 4:20-22 *(TPT)*:

Listen carefully, my dear child, to everything that I teach you, and pay attention to all that I have to say. 21 Fill your thoughts with my words until they penetrate deep into your spirit. 22 Then, as you unwrap my words, they will impart true life and radiant health into the very core of your being. 23 So above all, guard the affections of your heart, for they affect all that you are. Pay attention to the welfare of your innermost being, for from there flows the wellspring of life.

John 4:14 *(TPT)*:

But if anyone drinks the living water I give them, they will never thirst again and will be forever satisfied! For when you drink the water I give you it becomes a gushing fountain of the Holy Spirit, springing up and flooding you with endless life!

Have you ever felt dissatisfied with yourself or your life? Have you ever looked outside of Him to find satisfaction? True satisfaction and fulfillment is only found when we choose Jesus and let His love define our lives. Write down how His words of love spoke to your heart today.

_____

_____

_____

_____

_____

_____

_____

_____

_____

_____

_____

_____

_____

_____

_____

_____

_____

_____

_____

_____

_____

Jesus, I choose You to fulfill the longings of my heart to be unconditionally loved, approved and accepted. You chose me as the focus of Your love, to be made whole and holy by Your love. I will let Your love define who I truly am! I receive Your love for me today.

– Your beloved Bride

Day 3

Let Me Encourage Your Heart

Good morning, My love,

When you feel unworthy or in need, I'll always remind you that you're so lovely to Me! When the lies of the enemy make you feel dark in your soul, remember, it's My love that makes you whole.

Listen closely to what I say: You are beautiful in every way! You are not a victim of your circumstances. You're not defined by your past. You are my victorious bride, arising from the ashes to a brand-new life. The world has lost its power to define you, for you are one with Me. Everything I am, and everything I have, is yours, for I am your true identity!

When the voice of the enemy tells you that you're not good enough or you lack in some way, turn toward Me, and let me smother you with my Spirit-kiss divine. Remember, My love, you're not his, you are Mine! I chose you to be My beloved bride. I clothed you in my righteousness and you are without fault in My eyes. You're important and valuable and worthy; it's true. You are worth the price I paid for you. My radiant one, I believe in you!

– Your Bridegroom, Jesus

Song of Songs 1:5 (TPT):

__The Shulamite__ ... In this twilight darkness I know I am so unworthy—so in need. __The Shepherd-King__ Yet you are so lovely! __The Shulamite__ I feel as dark and dry as the desert tents of the wandering nomads. __The Shepherd-King__ Yet you are so lovely—like the fine linen tapestry hanging in the Holy Place.

Romans 8:1 (TPT):

So now the case is closed. There remains no accusing voice of condemnation against those who are joined in life-union with Jesus, the Anointed One.

Song of Songs 2:16 (TPT):

I know my lover is mine and I have everything in you, for we delight ourselves in each other.

Isaiah 61:10 (TLB):

Let me tell you how happy God has made me! For he has clothed me with garments of salvation and draped about me the robe of righteousness. I am like a bridegroom in his wedding suit or a bride with her jewels.

Have you ever felt unworthy or not good enough? What does Jesus say when you feel this way? Write down what He said in today's devotion that particularly touched your heart.

_____

_____

_____

_____

_____

_____

_____

_____

_____

_____

_____

_____

_____

_____

_____

_____

_____

_____

_____

_____

_____

_____

Jesus, when I feel dark in my soul, it's Your love that makes me whole. When the enemy tells me that I'm not good enough, I will turn toward You and let You smother me with Your Spirit-kiss divine. You've clothed me in Your righteousness, and I am without fault in Your eyes. Thank You for loving me!

– Your beloved Bride

Day 4

I Did Not Create You to Live in Stress

Good morning, My love,

If you ever feel overwhelmed by all the things you need to do, remember, I live inside of you! Come to Me, My love, and sit down and rest. I did not create you to live in stress. I made you My bride. I gave you My peace, so turn your focus from you to Me! Listen to My voice- and hear Me say, "Your value is not determined by what you accomplish today."

I know there are important things you need to do. Don't listen to the lie that you are inadequate because that's not true. When you feel weak, I will make you strong; for My grace is sufficient for you! Look to Me, My love, and remember that we are one. You have My power and My wisdom to accomplish what needs to be done. Knowing this will cause you to live freely and lightly every single day. Yes, you'll truly enjoy your life as you live in the unforced rhythms of My grace.

— Your Bridegroom, Jesus

Song of Songs 1:7 *(TPT)*:

Won't you tell me, lover of my soul, where do you feed your flock? Where do you lead your beloved ones to rest in the heat of the day? For I wish to be wrapped all around you as I wander among the flocks of your shepherds. It is you I long for, with no veil between us!

Matthew 6:6 *(MSG)*:

Here's what I want you to do: Find a quiet, secluded place so you won't be tempted to role-play before God. Just be there as simply and honestly as you can manage. The focus will shift from you to God, and you will begin to sense his grace.

2 Corinthians 12:9 *(MSG)*:

My grace is enough; it's all you need. My strength comes into its own in your weakness.

Matthew 11:28-30 *(MSG)*:

28-30 Are you tired? Worn out? Burned out on religion? Come to me. Get away with me and you'll recover your life. I'll show you how to take a real rest. Walk with me and work with me—watch how I do it. Learn the unforced rhythms of grace. I won't lay anything heavy or ill-fitting on you. Keep company with me and you'll learn to live freely and lightly.

Have you ever felt overwhelmed by all the things you need to do? What did Jesus speak to you in today's devotion to encourage your heart when you feel this way?

_____

_____

_____

_____

_____

_____

_____

_____

_____

_____

_____

_____

_____

_____

_____

_____

_____

_____

_____

_____

_____

_____

_____

Jesus, when I feel overwhelmed by all the things
I need to do, I will look to You as My strength and
My wisdom. I am one with You, so I have everything
I need to accomplish what needs to be done. Help
me to live freely and lightly in Your love for me.

– Your beloved Bride

Day 5
I Will Take Care of Your Concerns

Good morning, My love,

I have loved you and cared for you since the day you were born. I made you and it delights My heart to take care of you. Listen, My radiant one, if you ever lose sight of Me and begin to feel worried or anxious, just remember how much I love you!

I am your Prince of Peace. Come to me with your burdens and cares and let Me remind you how I see you. When I look at you, I see royalty, and you are so thrilling to Me. Just call out My name, for I am always here to help you! I care about you, My love, and I watch over you every moment of every day.

When the cares of life try to weigh on you today, simply rest in Me, and remember My promises to you. My perfect love will cast out all your fears. You have no need to worry, My love, for I will take care of every concern of your heart so that you can enjoy My perfect and constant peace!

– Your Bridegroom, Jesus

Song of Songs 1:8-9 *(TPT)*:

8 Listen, my radiant one—if you ever lose sight of me, just follow in my footsteps where I lead my lovers. Come with your burdens and cares. Come to the place near the sanctuary of my shepherds. 9 My dearest one, let me tell you how I see you—you are so thrilling to me.

ISAIAH 46:3-4 *(TLB)*:

3...I have created you and cared for you since you were born. 4 I will be your God through all your lifetime, yes, even when your hair is white with age. I made you and I will care for you. I will carry you along and be your Savior.

1 Peter 5:7 *(AMPC)*:

Casting the whole of your care [all your anxieties, all your worries, all your concerns, once and for all] on Him, for He cares for you affectionately and cares about you watchfully.

Psalm 138:8 *(NKJV)*:

The Lord will perfect that which concerns me...

Psalm 55:22 (TPT):

So here's what I've learned through it all: Leave all your cares and anxieties at the feet of the Lord, and measureless grace will strengthen you.

Have you had concerns in your heart lately? Take time to talk to Jesus about them. Write down what Jesus said in today's devotion that particularly touched your heart and brought you peace.

_____

_____

_____

_____

_____

_____

_____

_____

_____

_____

_____

_____

_____

_____

_____

_____

_____

_____

_____

_____

_____

_____

_____

Jesus, when the cares of life weigh on me, I
will give them to You and remember Your promises
to me. Your perfect love sets my heart free from all
fear. Thank You for taking care of everything that
concerns me. I will rest in Your love today!

– Your beloved Bride

Day 6

My Resurrection Is Your Resurrection, Too!

Good morning, My love,

Today I want to remind you how deeply you are loved! You were worth the suffering I endured on the cross. You were the joy set before me. You were My prize. You were the reason I laid down My life. I paid the ultimate price to make you My bride. There is nothing greater I could do to prove My incredible love for you!

When I died, you died with Me, and when I rose from the dead, we were raised together victoriously! When the price was paid, the earth began to shake, and the power of love raised us from the grave! My resurrection is your resurrection, too! My greatest desire has always been to be one with You.

I conquered sin and death and rescued you from fear and shame. No guilt, no shame, no fear, no dread can hold you captive any longer. Your mistakes and the world around you can no longer define who you are. You must only believe that your true identity is now found in Me!

You're forgiven, My love; you're righteous and pure. You're My beautiful, perfect, and holy bride. I am your conquering King, and now and forever, you reign as one with Me!

– Your Bridegroom, Jesus

Song of Songs 1:12-13 *(TPT)*:

12 As the king surrounded me at his table, the sweet fragrance of my praise perfume awakened the night. 13 A sachet of myrrh is my lover, like a tied-up bundle of myrrh resting over my heart.

Hebrews 12:2 *(NCV)*:

Let us look only to Jesus, the One who began our faith and who makes it perfect. He suffered death on the cross. But he accepted the shame as if it were nothing because of the joy that God put before him. And now he is sitting at the right side of God's throne.

Romans 6:4 *(TPT)*:

Sharing in his death by our baptism means that we were co-buried and entombed with him, so that when the Father's glory raised Christ from the dead, we were also raised with him. We have been co-resurrected with him so that we could be empowered to walk in the freshness of new life.

Colossians 3:1 *(TPT)*:

Christ's resurrection is your resurrection too...

Galatians 2:20 *(TPT)*:

My old identity has been co-crucified with Messiah and no longer lives; for the nails of his cross crucified me with him. And now the essence of this new life is no longer mine, for the Anointed One lives his life through me—we live in union as one! My new life is empowered by the faith of the Son of God who loves me so much that he gave himself for me, and dispenses his life into mine!

How did Jesus prove His great love for you? Write down what He said in today's devotion that particularly touched your heart.

_____

_____

_____

_____

_____

_____

_____

_____

_____

_____

_____

_____

_____

_____

_____

_____

_____

_____

_____

_____

_____

_____

Jesus, oh how You love me! My old identity was crucified with You, and we were raised together so that I can walk in the power of a new life. Your resurrection is my resurrection, too. I am forgiven, righteous, and holy because of You. My true identity is now found in you!

– Your beloved Bride

Day 7

Be Secure in My Opinion of You

Good morning, My love,

I want you to live confident and secure in My love and opinion of you. My love for you is unconditional. No matter what you do, I will never change how I think of you! I want you to live free from the fear of what others think. When you value the opinions of others more than you value Mine, it will cause you to live fearfully and insecure.

Don't you see, My love? What others think of you does not determine your value or worth. Their opinions do not define who you are, for your identity is found in My opinion of you! You are My amazing and wonderful bride, and there is nothing at all wrong with you.

When you believe what I say is true, that's when it won't matter anymore what others think about you. No longer held captive by fear of human opinion, you'll truly live free! Yes, My love, you'll live confident and secure in your true identity!

– Your Bridegroom, Jesus

John 5:44 (AMPC):

How is it possible for you to believe [how can you learn to believe], you who [are content to seek and] receive praise and honor and glory from one another, and yet do not seek the praise and honor and glory which come from Him Who alone is God?

Proverbs 29:25 (MSG):

The fear of human opinion disables; trusting in GOD protects you from that.

Song of Songs 2:3-4 (TPT):

3 My beloved is to me the most fragrant apple tree—he stands above the sons of men. Sitting under his grace-shadow, I blossom in his shade, enjoying the sweet taste of his pleasant, delicious fruit, resting with delight where his glory never fades. 4 Suddenly, he transported me into his house of wine—he looked upon me with his unrelenting love divine.

Psalm 139:14 (NCV):

I praise you because you made me in an amazing and wonderful way. What you have done is wonderful. I know this very well.

Psalm 139:17 (TPT):

Every single moment you are thinking of me! How precious and wonderful to consider that you cherish me constantly in your every thought!

Have you ever been afraid of what others think of you? Has the fear of human opinion ever held you back? Write down what Jesus spoke to you in today's devotion that particularly touched your heart.

_____

_____

_____

_____

_____

_____

_____

_____

_____

_____

_____

_____

_____

_____

_____

_____

_____

_____

_____

_____

_____

_____

_____

_____

_____

Jesus, today I choose to value Your opinion of me above everyone else's. You say I am amazing and wonderful and that there is nothing wrong with me. Help me to live free from the fear of what others think. My value is found in You!

– Your beloved Bride

Day 8
I Will Rescue Your Children

Good morning, My love,

I want to remind you today that your children are My children, too. I know some of their choices have made your heart sad, but listen to Me, My love, hear what I say. Let My words of life make your heart glad today!

I know you want to fix them with all the things you've tried to do. But remember, I am not only their Father, but their Savior, too. I know how to rescue them from all the lies they've believed. I promised to teach them and give them great peace. So, rest in My love and leave the fixing to Me.

I will turn their ashes into beauty, their sadness into joy, and their despair into songs of praise. I will contend with those who contend with them, and our children I will save! Don't be distracted by what you see. Turn your focus from them to Me. Use your authority, as My beloved bride, and declare what I say over their lives.

My Spirit will not leave them, for I am at work, creating in their hearts the desire and power to do what is right. No devil in hell can stop it from happening. I know their lives from beginning to end. And I want to remind you, My bride, that we win! Our children will shine with My glory for the world to see. And you will enjoy My peace as you rest in Me!

– Your Bridegroom, Jesus

Song of Songs 2:6 *(TPT)*:

His left hand cradles my head while his right hand holds me close. I'm at rest in this love.

Isaiah 54:10, 13 *(NLT)*:

10 "...My covenant of blessing will never be broken," says the LORD, who has mercy on you... 13 "I will teach all your children, and they will enjoy great peace."

Isaiah 61:3 *(NCV)*:

...I will give them a crown to replace their ashes, and the oil of gladness to replace their sorrow, and clothes of praise to replace their spirit of sadness. Then they will be called Trees of Goodness, trees planted by the LORD to show his greatness.

Isaiah 49:23, 25 *(NIV)*:

23...Then you will know that I am the LORD; those who hope in me will not be disappointed.

25...I will contend with those who contend with you, and your children I will save.

Isaiah 59:21 *(NLT)*:

"And this is my covenant with them," says the LORD. "My Spirit will not leave them, and neither will these words I have given you. They will be on your lips and on the lips of your children and your children's children forever. I, the LORD, have spoken!"

Proverbs 11:21 *(TLB)*:

...You can also be very sure God will rescue the children of the godly.

Have you had some concerns about your children lately? How did the promises that Jesus spoke to your heart today encourage you? Which ones ministered to your heart the most? Take some time today to speak His Word over your children.

_____

_____

_____

_____

_____

_____

_____

_____

_____

_____

_____

_____

_____

_____

_____

_____

_____

_____

_____

_____

_____

_____

_____

Jesus, thank You for reminding me that my children are Your children, too. You will teach them and they will enjoy great peace. I give them to You, and I trust You to work out Your good plan for their lives. Your promises are true, and I will rest in You!

– Your beloved Bride

Day 9
We Will Do it Together

Good morning, My love,

Arise, My beautiful one, and come away with Me! I have come as you have asked to set your heart free. I come to the places where you are hiding behind the lies you've believed. The season of hiding is over and gone! Now is the time, My love, to arise. It's time for those barren places to start bearing fruit in your life. There are things I speak over you that you have yet to see. It's time for you to say, "Yes!" My love, and let go of all the lies you've believed:

– I'm not good enough
– I can't do it
– It's too hard
– There's something wrong with me

They're all lies, My love, can't you see? Negative thoughts are troubling foxes within your soul that have hindered what I say about you from coming forth in your life. It's time for us to get rid of all the lies. You must catch those troubling foxes, those sly little foxes that hinder our relationship. They are lies of the enemy that are intended to ruin what I've planted within you. Will you catch them and remove them for Me? We will do it together, My beautiful bride! When I speak words of life to you, simply say, "Yes!" to Me. And the purpose and plans I have for your life will spring forth for all to see!

– Your Bridegroom, Jesus

Song of Songs 2:8-15 (TPT):

The Shulamite *8Listen! I hear my lover's voice. I know it's him coming to me—leaping with joy over mountains, skipping in love over the hills that separate us, to come to me. 9Let me describe him: he is graceful as a gazelle, swift as a wild stag. Now he comes closer, even to the places where I hide. He gazes into my soul, peering through the portal as he blossoms within my heart. 10The one I love calls to me:*

The Bridegroom-King *Arise, my dearest. Hurry, my darling. Come away with me! I have come as you have asked to draw you to my heart and lead you out. For now is the time, my beautiful one. 11The season has changed, the bondage of your barren winter has ended, and the season of hiding is over and gone. The rains have soaked the earth. 12and left it bright with blossoming flowers. The season for singing and pruning the vines has arrived. I hear the cooing of doves in our land, filling the air with songs to awaken you and guide you forth. 13Can you not discern this new day of destiny breaking forth around you? The early signs of my purposes and plans are bursting forth. The budding vines of new life are now blooming everywhere. The fragrance of their flowers whispers, "There is change in the air." Arise, my love, my beautiful companion, and run with me to the higher place. For now is the time to arise and come away with me. 14For you are my dove, hidden in the split-open rock. It was I who took you and hid you up high in the secret stairway of the sky. Let me see your radiant face and hear your sweet voice. How beautiful your eyes of worship and lovely your voice in prayer. 15You must catch the troubling foxes, those sly little foxes that hinder our relationship. For they raid our budding vineyard of love to ruin what I've planted within you. Will you catch them and remove them for me? We will do it together.*

Jesus comes to the places in your heart where you've hidden behind lies that have brought fear and shame to your heart. He comes to set your heart free with the truth of His love. Write down what Jesus spoke to you in today's devotion that particularly touched your heart.

_____

_____

_____

_____

_____

_____

_____

_____

_____

_____

_____

_____

_____

_____

_____

_____

_____

_____

_____

_____

_____

_____

_____

Jesus, thank You for coming to the places where I hide behind fear and shame, to set me free with Your great love. It gives me such peace to know that I don't have to catch the troubling foxes and get rid them on my own. We will do it together!

– Your beloved Bride

Day 10
I Will Rescue You!

Good morning, My love,

I know there are times your heart has been troubled and you've wondered, "Where are you Lord?" But remember, My love, I live inside of you, so I am always with you. I hear your cry for help, and I will rescue you. When you feel overwhelmed by the cares of life, don't trust in your own ability to fix the problem. Instead, turn your thoughts toward Me and remember My great love for you! You'll find and feel my presence even in your time of pressure and trouble.

"Don't be afraid, I've redeemed you. I've called your name. You're mine. When you're in over your head, I'll be there with you. When you're in rough waters, you will not go down. When you're between a rock and a hard place, it won't be a dead end—Because I am GOD, your personal God, The Holy of Israel, your Savior. I paid a huge price for you…That's how much you mean to me! That's how much I love you! I'd sell off the whole world to get you back, trade the creation just for you" (Isaiah 43:1-3 MSG).

I'll be your glorious hero! You'll be amazed at all that I do for you, and you'll enjoy My salvation to the fullest. Always remember, I love you. You can trust Me. I got this! For I am your Savior, and I will rescue you as many times as you need to be rescued!

– Your Bridegroom, Jesus

Song of Songs 3:1, 7-8 *(TPT)*:

1 Night after night I'm tossing and turning on my bed of travail. Why did I let him go from me? How my heart now aches for him, but he is nowhere to be found!... 7 Look! It is the king's marriage carriage. The love seat surrounded by sixty champions, the mightiest of Israel's host, are like pillars of protection. 8 They are angelic warriors standing ready with swords to defend the king and his fiancée from every terror of the night.

2 Corinthians 1:8-11 *(MSG)*:

We don't want you in the dark, friends, about how hard it was when all this came down on us in Asia province. It was so bad we didn't think we were going to make it... Instead of trusting in our own strength or wits to get out of it, we were forced to trust God totally—not a bad idea since he's the God who raises the dead! And he did it, rescued us from certain doom. And he'll do it again, rescuing us as many times as we need rescuing...

Isaiah 41:13 *(NIV)*:

For I am the LORD, your God who takes hold of your right hand and says to you, Do not fear; I will help you.

Psalm 91:15-16 *(TPT)*:

15 I will answer your cry for help every time you pray, and you will find and feel my presence even in your time of pressure and trouble. I will be your glorious hero and give you a feast. 16 You will be satisfied with a full life and with all that I do for you. For you will enjoy the fullness of my salvation!

Isaiah 54:5 *(CEV)*:

The LORD All-Powerful, the Holy God of Israel, rules all the earth. He is your Creator and husband, and he will rescue you.

Have you ever wondered, "Where are you Lord?" Have you ever cried for help and felt like He wasn't helping you? Take some time to write down a particular phrase in today's devotion that ministered to your heart.

_____

_____

_____

_____

_____

_____

_____

_____

_____

_____

_____

_____

_____

_____

_____

_____

_____

_____

_____

_____

_____

_____

Jesus, there have been times when I've wondered, "Where are You?" Thank You for reminding me that You are as close as You could ever be because You live inside of me. You are my glorious hero, and You will rescue me as many times as I need to be rescued!

– Your beloved Bride

Day 11
You Are One with Me

Good morning, My love,

I remember the day you became one with Me. I pursued you with My passionate, relentless love until your heart awakened and you could see. That was the day you said, "Yes!" to Me. You are everything I ever wanted. You are My prize. My dream came true the day you became My bride.

Ask Me to show you the truth that will set your heart free, and I will continue to unveil the height and depth of My perfect love which is revealed in the truth that you are one with Me! Yes, My perfect love will drive all fear from your heart, and the voice of accusation will lose its power to condemn you. You'll see My glory manifest in every area of your life; it's true! You'll begin to experience the power of My resurrection life in you!

You are one with perfect love! Yes, you are one with Me! I gave you My glory so the whole world could see. You are righteous, favored, and blessed because I gave you My identity! All you must do is receive. See yourself as My beloved bride, reigning as one with Me, and you'll experience My abundant life right now and for all eternity!

– Your Bridegroom, Jesus

Song of Songs 3:11 *(TPT)*:

Rise up, Zion maidens, brides-to-be! Come and feast your eyes on this king as he passes in procession on his way to his wedding. This is the day filled with overwhelming joy—the day of his great gladness.

Songs of Song 2:10 *(TPT)*:

Arise, my dearest. Hurry, my darling. Come away with me! I have come as you have asked to draw you to my heart and lead you out. For now is the time, my beautiful one.

John 17:20-23 *(TPT)*:

²⁰ And I ask not only for these disciples, but also for all those who will one day believe in me through their message. ²¹ I pray for them all to be joined together as one even as you and I, Father, are joined together as one. I pray for them to become one with us so that the world will recognize that you sent me. ²² For the very glory you have given to me I have given them so that they will be joined together as one and experience the same unity that we enjoy. ²³ You live fully in me and now I live fully in them so that they will experience perfect unity, and the world will be convinced that you have sent me, for they will see that you love each one of them with the same passionate love that you have for me.

Philippians 3:10-11 (TPT):

¹⁰ And I continually long to know the wonders of Jesus more fully and to experience the overflowing power of his resurrection working in me. I will be one with him in his sufferings and I will be one with him in his death. ¹¹ Only then will I be able to experience complete oneness with him in his resurrection from the realm of death.

Can you see Jesus' passionate love for you in today's devotion? Take some time to write down a particular phrase that ministered to your heart. What did Jesus pray for you in John 17:20-23?

_____

_____

_____

_____

_____

_____

_____

_____

_____

_____

_____

_____

_____

_____

_____

_____

_____

_____

_____

_____

_____

Jesus, I said, "Yes!" to You and now You're one with me. I ask You to show me the truth that will set my heart free. I want to know You more fully and experience the power outflowing from Your resurrection. I am righteous, favored and blessed because You gave me Your identity.

– Your beloved Bride

Day 12
You Are Valuable

Good morning, My love,

Today I want to remind you just how valuable you are. The world looks to their accomplishments, appearance, and social status to determine their worth. The world's system is about measuring your value by what you do and the opinions of others. Please don't do that, My love. Your value is not defined by any of those things. Your value was determined by the price I paid for you. I gave My life in exchange for you!

Never believe the lie that you are less valuable than anyone else. Looking outside of Me to determine your value only causes you to compare yourself to others. I redeemed you from that fruitless way of living.

When I look at you, I see My treasure, My bride. I see My pearl of great price. You are like fine tapestry – an original work of art – My most magnificent masterpiece. You are beauty itself to Me! You are worthy of love! You deserve honor and respect, so don't settle for anything less! I long to hear you say, "Jesus, I am valuable, important, and special. I know it's true! My value is found in you."

You never need to worry, My love. You are more valuable to Me than anything else in this world. When you find your value in Me, your heart will be truly free!

– Your Bridegroom, Jesus

45

Song of Songs 4:1 *(TPT)*:

Listen, my dearest darling, you are so beautiful—you are beauty itself to me!

Song of Songs 7:1 *(TPT)*:

...You are truly the poetry of God—his very handiwork.

1 Peter 1:18-19 *(AMPC)*:

18 You must know (recognize) that you were redeemed (ransomed) from the useless (fruitless) way of living inherited by tradition from [your] forefathers, not with corruptible things [such as] silver and gold, 19 But [you were purchased] with the precious blood of Christ (the Messiah), like that of a [sacrificial] lamb without blemish or spot.

Luke 12:6-7 *(TPT)*:

What is the value of your soul to God? Could your worth be defined by an amount of money? God doesn't abandon or forget even the small sparrow he has made. How then could he forget or abandon you? What about the seemingly minor issues of your life? Do they matter to God? Of course they do! So you never need to worry, for you are more valuable to God than anything else in this world.

Galatians 5:25-26 *(MSG)*:

Since this is the kind of life we have chosen, the life of the Spirit, let us make sure that we do not just hold it as an idea in our heads or a sentiment in our hearts, but work out its implications in every detail of our lives. That means we will not compare ourselves with each other as if one of us were better and another worse. We have far more interesting things to do with our lives. Each of us is an original.

Have you ever looked to your accomplishments, appearance, or other people's opinions to determine your value or worth? Have you ever compared yourself to others? What did that produce in your heart? Take time today to talk to Jesus about your value, and write down a particular phrase or verse that ministered to your heart.

_____

_____

_____

_____

_____

_____

_____

_____

_____

_____

_____

_____

_____

_____

_____

_____

_____

_____

_____

_____

_____

Jesus, thank You for reminding me of the huge price You paid for me. I am Your treasure, Your pearl of great price, Your most magnificent masterpiece. I'm valuable, important and special; I know it's true! My value is found in You! Thank You for loving me.

– Your beloved Bride

Day 13

Let Me Hear Your Sweet Voice

Good morning, My love,

When I hear you speak in agreement with Me, it makes Me so happy to see you receive. Don't believe the lie that it's prideful when you agree with what I say about you. I said what My Father said about Me, even though others thought I was prideful, too. But listen, My love: giving up your own opinion of yourself for Mine is the most yielded sacrifice you could ever make for Me. That, My love, is true humility.

My love song over you is a beautiful melody. So, sing, My love. Let Me hear your sweet voice. Receive My love today, and let Me hear you say:

Jesus, I know You love me, so with You I agree. I am valuable, accepted, and approved! I am forgiven, worthy and favored, it's true! I am led by Your Spirit, abundantly blessed, and clothed in Your righteousness. I stand before You without a single fault, free from all fear and shame. I believe You when You say my sins are washed away! Beauty is what You see when You look at Me!

Oh, My love, the words of your mouth are as refreshing as an oasis. What pleasure you bring to Me! You're speaking words of mercy and grace. When you declare what I say, you'll experience the power outflowing from My resurrection as new life springs forth. Yes, My love, you choose life when you declare your worth!

– Your Bridegroom, Jesus

Song of Songs 4:3 *(TPT)*:

Your lips are as lovely as Rahab's scarlet ribbon, speaking mercy, speaking grace. The words of your mouth are as refreshing as an oasis. What pleasure you bring to me! I see your blushing cheeks opened like the halves of a pomegranate, showing through your veil of tender meekness.

Song of Songs 6:5-7 *(TPT)*:

5 Turn your eyes from me; I can't take it anymore! I can't resist the passion of these eyes that I adore. Overpowered by a glance, my ravished heart— undone. Held captive by your love, I am truly overcome! For your undying devotion to me is the most yielded sacrifice. 6 The shining of your spirit shows how you have taken my truth to become balanced and complete. 7 Your beautiful blushing cheeks reveal how real your passion is for me, even hidden behind your veil of humility.

Hebrews 10:9-10, 14 *(TPT)*:

9 And then he said, "God, I will be the One to go and do your will." So by being the sacrifice that removes sin, he abolishes animal sacrifices and replaces that entire system with the new covenant. 10 By God's will we have been purified and made holy once and for all through the sacrifice of the body of Jesus, the Messiah!

14 And by his one perfect sacrifice he made us perfectly holy and complete for all time!

Proverbs 4:10 *(TPT)*:

...If you will take the time to stop and listen to me and embrace what I say, you will live a long and happy life full of understanding in every way.

Jesus loves to hear your sweet voice, receiving His love, and agreeing with what He says about you. Take time today to write down what spoke to your heart from today's devotion.

_____
_____
_____
_____
_____
_____
_____
_____
_____
_____
_____
_____
_____
_____
_____
_____
_____
_____
_____
_____
_____
_____

Jesus, I will humbly embrace what You say about me. I give up my opinion of myself for Yours. I want to experience the power outflowing from Your resurrection, so I choose life today by declaring My worth! You are my Husband and I am one with You!

– Your beloved Bride

Day 14
Your Future is Secure

Good morning, My love,

There are many things in this world that can tempt your heart to be concerned about your future, but I want you to live confident and secure in My great love for you! My plan has always been to prosper you, and to give you the future you hope for. I'm always working things together for your good. I will crown your year with my goodness and every step you take will be blessed with abundance!

When negative thoughts about your future come to your mind and try to fill your heart with fear, remember who you are! You are my righteous bride, and you have my resurrection life. You are blessed abundantly, and you reign as one with me!

Strength and dignity are your clothing, and your position is strong and secure! Your future is bright, My love, so live adventurously expectant of all the good that is coming because I have given you a glorious inheritance, and your future is secure in Me!

– Your Bridegroom, Jesus

Song of Songs 4:4 *(TPT)*:

When I look at you, I see your inner strength, so stately and strong. You are as secure as David's fortress...

Proverbs 31:25 *(AMPC)*:

Strength and dignity are her clothing and her position is strong and secure; she rejoices over the future...

Jeremiah 29:11 *(MSG)*:

I know what I'm doing. I have it all planned out—plans to take care of you, not abandon you, plans to give you the future you hope for.

Romans 8:28 *(MSG)*:

That's why we can be so sure that every detail in our lives of love for God is worked into something good.

Psalm 65:11 *(NKJV)*:

You crown the year with Your goodness, And Your paths drip with abundance.

Romans 8:15-16 *(MSG)*:

This resurrection life you received from God is not a timid, grave-tending life. It's adventurously expectant, greeting God with a childlike "What's next, Papa?" God's Spirit touches our spirits and confirms who we really are. We know who he is, and we know who we are: Father and children. And we know we are going to get what's coming to us—an unbelievable inheritance!

Have you ever worried about your future? Jesus' words of love always bring peace to our hearts. Take time to write down what ministered to your heart from today's devotional.

_____
_____
_____
_____
_____
_____
_____
_____
_____
_____
_____
_____
_____
_____
_____
_____
_____
_____
_____
_____
_____
_____
_____
_____

Jesus, Your plan is to prosper me. You work everything together for my good. I am Your righteous bride, and I have Your resurrection life. I rejoice over my future because it is secure in You.

– Your beloved Bride

Day 15
There Is Nothing Wrong with You!

Good morning, My love,

It delights My heart to sing over you! Every day and all day long, you are the theme of My song. I rejoice over you with singing, and with songs of love, I will calm all your fears. You are the desire of My heart! You are My dream come true. I love everything about you! Don't believe the lie that there is something wrong with you.

I chose you to be my beloved bride. You are holy and without fault in My eyes! My darling, everything about you is beautiful, and there is nothing at all wrong with you. You're beautiful from head to toe, My dear love, beautiful beyond compare and absolutely flawless!

When you said, "Yes!" to Me, I brought you to the Father and presented you as My pure and faultless bride with unspeakable, ecstatic delight! You've captured My heart. You looked at me, and I fell in love. One look my way and I was hopelessly in love. Believe Me when I say, "You're perfect in every way!" Rest in my love today.

– Your Bridegroom, Jesus

Song of Songs 2:1-2 *(TPT)*:

¹ I'm truly His rose, the very theme of his song. I'm overshadowed by his love, growing in the valley! **The Shepherd-King** *² Yes, you are my darling companion.*

Zephaniah 3:17 *(NLT)*:

For the LORD your God is living among you. He is a mighty savior. He will take delight in you with gladness. With his love, he will calm all your fears. He will rejoice over you with joyful songs.

Song of Songs 4:7 *(NCV)*:

My darling, everything about you is beautiful, and there is nothing at all wrong with you.

Song of Songs 4:9 *(MSG)*:

You've captured my heart, dear friend. You looked at me, and I fell in love. One look my way and I was hopelessly in love!

Jude 1:24 *(AMPC)*:

Now to Him Who is able to keep you without stumbling or slipping or falling, and to present [you] unblemished (blameless and faultless) before the presence of His glory in triumphant joy and exultation [with unspeakable, ecstatic delight].

Take a moment to think upon the truth that Jesus spoke to your heart today. Have you ever believed the lie that there is something wrong with you? How did Jesus' words of love and truth about you affect your heart? Share your thoughts with Him.

_____
_____
_____
_____
_____
_____
_____
_____
_____
_____
_____
_____
_____
_____
_____
_____
_____
_____
_____
_____
_____
_____

Jesus, You chose me to be Your beloved bride.
I am holy and without fault in Your eyes. What You
say about me is true. Everything about me is beautiful,
and there is nothing at all wrong with Me. I will
rest in Your love today!

– Your beloved Bride

Day 16

Now You're Ready to Reign, My Bride!

Good morning, My love,

Despite the unanswered questions, and the doubts and fears within your heart, you've made up your mind and said, "Yes!" to Me. Instead of pushing My love away, you've chosen to receive. You said, "Yes, I'll be Your bride!" And now you're ready, My love, to reign as one with Me!

We're seated together in heavenly places, in the place of victory, far above the enemy's lies. You'll recognize them quickly, My love, and they won't be able to hide. You'll expose them to the light of My love, and they'll dissipate before your eyes. Together we'll enforce the defeat of the enemy. Now you'll live free from all the accusing voices you were tempted to believe. You sit far above the enemy and all his schemes, for he is under your feet. Now's the time, My love, to declare My victory.

Your prayers are powerful and effective, for you are My righteous bride. I've given you My authority to confidently declare what I say over your life. When you speak with authority and thank Me for My promises to you, it's the highest form of worship you could ever offer Me. That's when I feel your greatest love for Me!

Your loving words are like milk and honey, for I find the promised land flowing from within you. For now My words are your words, too! Oh, My love, it's so beautiful to see, when you reign as one with Me!

– Your Bridegroom, Jesus

Song of Songs 2:6-11 *(TPT)*:

The Shulamite *6* *I've made up my mind. Until the darkness disappears and the dawn has fully come, in spite of shadows and fears, I will go to the mountaintop with you—the mountain of suffering love and the hill of burning incense. Yes, I will be your bride.* **The Bridegroom-King** *7* *Every part of you is so beautiful, my darling. Perfect is your beauty, without flaw within.* *8* *Now you are ready, my bride, to come with me as we climb the highest peaks together. Come with me through the archway of trust. We will look down from the crest of the glistening mounts and from the summit of our sublime sanctuary. Together we will wage war in the lion's den and the leopard's lair as they watch nightly for their prey.* *9* *I am held hostage by your love and by the graces of righteousness shining upon you.* *10* *How satisfying to me, my equal, my bride. Your love is my finest wine—intoxicating and thrilling. And your sweet, perfumed praises—so exotic, so pleasing.* *11* *Your loving words are like the honey-comb to me; your tongue releases milk and honey, for I find the Promised Land flowing within you.*

Luke 10:19 *(AMPC)*:

Behold! I have given you authority and power to trample upon serpents and scorpions, and [physical and mental strength and ability] over all the power that the enemy [possesses]; and nothing shall in any way harm you.

Ephesians 2:6 *(TPT)*:

He raised us up with Christ the exalted One, and we ascended with him into the glorious perfection and authority of the heavenly realm, for we are now co-seated as one with Christ!

Jesus has given you the authority, as His beloved bride, to speak His truth over your life. Take time today to write down and declare what He says about you, and reign as one with Him.

_____

_____

_____

_____

_____

_____

_____

_____

_____

_____

_____

_____

_____

_____

_____

_____

_____

_____

_____

_____

Jesus, I say, "Yes! I will be Your bride!" I am seated with You, far above the enemy and all his lies. Now and forever I will reign as one with You as I declare Your truth over my life. Thank You for Your promises to me. Your love has set me free!

– Your beloved Bride

Day 17

You Are My Paradise Garden

Good morning, My love,

You are My darling bride, My private paradise, fastened to My heart. When I look at you, I see a reflection of Me. I see My perfect righteousness when I look at your face, for it was My gift to you on our wedding day. That was the moment you became one with Me; for I gave you My very identity. Yes, I gave you My peace as a gift of My grace. I chose to live in you. For, you, My bride, are My holy place.

You are My paradise garden, a perfect partner for Me. Your inward life is now sprouting, bringing forth fruit. What a beautiful paradise unfolds within you. You opened your heart to Me, and let Me live My life through you. You have become an encouragement to others. Now your life is a living testimony that My Word is true!

Many clusters of my exquisite fruit now grow within your inner garden. Love, joy, peace, and confidence are springing forth. Kindness, goodness, and humility are what I see. A well of living water springs up from within you, like a mountain brook flowing into My heart. I see the fruit of My life in you!

— Your Bridegroom, Jesus

Song of Songs 4:12-16 *(TPT)*:

The Bridegroom-King *¹² My darling bride, my private paradise, fastened to my heart. A secret spring are you that no one else can have—my bubbling fountain hidden from public view. What a perfect partner to me now that I have you. ¹³⁻¹⁴ Your inward life is now sprouting, bringing forth fruit. What a beautiful paradise unfolds within you. When I'm near you, I smell aromas of the finest spice, for many clusters of my exquisite fruit now grow within your inner garden...¹⁵ Your life flows into mine, pure as a garden spring. A well of living water springs up from within you, like a mountain brook flowing into my heart!* ***The Shulamite Bride*** *¹⁶ Then may your awakening breath blow upon my life until I am fully yours. Breathe upon me with your Spirit wind. Stir up the sweet spice of your life within me. Spare nothing as you make me your fruitful garden. Hold nothing back until I release your fragrance. Come walk with me as you walked with Adam in your paradise garden. Come taste the fruits of your life in me.* ***The Bridegroom-King*** *I have come to you, my darling bride, for you are my paradise garden!*

John 15:5 *(TPT)*:

I am the sprouting vine and you're my branches. As you live in union with me as your source, fruitfulness will stream from within you...

Galatians 5:22-23 *(NLT)*:

₂₂ But the Holy Spirit produces this kind of fruit in our lives: love, joy, peace, patience, kindness, goodness, faithfulness, ₂₃ gentleness, and self-control..."

How does it make your heart feel to know that you are Jesus' private paradise? Take time to write down what spoke to your heart in today's devotional.

_____
_____
_____
_____
_____
_____
_____
_____
_____
_____
_____
_____
_____
_____
_____
_____
_____
_____
_____
_____
_____
_____
_____
_____

Jesus, thank You for giving me Your gift of righteousness. Spare nothing as You make me Your fruitful garden. I've opened my heart to You. Now live Your life through me.

– Your beloved Bride

Day 18

Open Your Heart Still Deeper to Me

Good morning, My love,

It's time to let go of the regrets, disappointments, and failures of your past. Let go of those things that didn't turn out like you'd hoped. Yes, My love, it's time to let them go. If you're ever tempted to define yourself by your past mistakes, turn your focus from you to Me, and listen to what I say: You're not a failure, My love, no matter how many mistakes you've made. You're perfect and flawless because you're one with Me!

I was beaten and crucified, but I won the victory! I conquered all the effects of death so you could share My life with Me. So, arise, My love, and open your heart still deeper to Me! When you hear Me speak, don't push My love away. Say, "Yes, I am who You say I am!" Agree with what I say! I'm creating in you the desire and power to do what is right. The same power that raised Me from the dead lives in you, My beloved bride. It's time for you to experience My resurrection life!

So arise, My love, from sadness, discouragement and pain. It's time to remember who you are! You're My victorious bride, and you're destined to reign! Fear of failure will never hold you back when you remember that I won, and you're one with Me! Believe that you're a success, My beautiful bride. Yes, arise and shine with My glory, and your true identity will spring forth for the whole world to see!

– Your Bridegroom, Jesus

Song of Songs 5:2-6 *(TPT)*:

The Shulamite Bride *² After this I let my devotion slumber, but my heart for him stayed awake. I had a dream. I dreamed of my beloved—he was coming to me in the darkness of night. The melody of the man I love awakened me. I heard his knock at my heart's door as he pleaded with me:* **The Bridegroom-King** *Arise, my love. Open your heart, my darling, deeper still to me. Will you receive me this dark night? There is no one else but you, my friend, my equal. I need you this night to arise and come be with me. You are my pure, loyal dove, a perfect partner for me. My flawless one, will you arise? For my heaviness and tears are more than I can bear. I have spent myself for you throughout the dark night.* **The Shulamite Bride** *³ I have already laid aside my own garments for you. How could I take them up again since I've yielded my righteousness to yours? You have cleansed my life and taken me so far. Isn't that enough? ⁴ My beloved reached into me to unlock my heart. The core of my very being trembled at his touch. How my soul melted when he spoke to me! ⁵ My spirit arose to open for more of his touch. As I surrendered to him, I began to sense his fragrance—the fragrance of his suffering love! It was the sense of myrrh flowing all through me!*

Isaiah 43:18; 25 *(NIV)*:

¹⁸ Forget the former things; do not dwell on the past... ²⁵ I, even I, am he who blots out your transgressions, for my own sake, and remembers your sins no more.

Isaiah 60:1-2 *(AMPC)*:

¹ Arise [from the depression and prostration in which circumstances have kept you—rise to a new life]! Shine (be radiant with the glory of the Lord), for your light has come, and the glory of the Lord has risen upon you! ² *For behold, darkness shall cover the earth, and dense darkness [all] peoples, but the Lord shall arise upon you... and His glory shall be seen on you.*

How does it make you feel to know that you are not defined by your failures? Do you have past regrets and disappointments that have held you captive to fear and shame? Talk to Jesus about what He spoke to you about this. Share your heart with Him today.

_____

_____

_____

_____

_____

_____

_____

_____

_____

_____

_____

_____

_____

_____

_____

_____

_____

_____

_____

_____

Jesus, today I open my heart still deeper to You. Heal my heart of the pain that is caused by the regrets and disappointments of my past. I won't push Your love away. I will arise and shine with Your glory. I am not a failure. I am a success because I am one with You. Thank You for loving me.

– Your beloved Bride,

Day 19

I Am the Healer of Your Heart

Good morning, My love,

I want you to live secure in my acceptance and approval. I know there are people who have judged you, said negative things about you, and even some who have walked away and rejected you. I know how you feel, My love, for I've been rejected, too. I know your heart has been hurt at times. I've seen the tears in your eyes, and I am here to comfort you. I am the Healer of your broken heart. I am the Lover of your soul. Only My love can truly make you whole!

Don't ever believe the lie that you are rejected and unwanted! Don't waste one moment thinking, "Why don't they want me?" You will never find peace in the answer to that question. You will only find pain. So, when your heart is hurting, turn your thoughts toward Me. Ask the question that brings healing to your heart and has the power to set you free, "Jesus, what do you say about me?"

You will hear Me whisper My love song into your heart, reminding you over and over again the truth of who you are. You are wonderful and good, My love, and I approve of you completely! I am your friend forever. I will never leave you nor reject you, no, not ever! So, believe Me when I say, "You're fully accepted in Me!" Then you will live secure in your true identity.

– Your Bridegroom, Jesus!

Song of Songs 5:7, 13, 16 (TPT):

7 As I walked throughout the city in search of him, the overseers stopped me as they made their rounds. They beat me and bruised me until I could take no more. They wounded me deeply and removed their covering from me.

13 Looking at his gentle face I see such fullness of emotion. Like a lovely garden where fragrant spices grow—what a man! No one speaks words so anointed as this one—words that both pierce and heal, words like lilies dripping with myrrh.

16 Most sweet are his kisses, even his whispers of love. He is delightful in every way and perfect from every viewpoint. If you ask me why I love him so, O brides-to-be, it's because there is none like him to me. Everything about him fills me with holy desire! And now he is my beloved—my friend forever.

Psalm 147:3 (AMP):

He heals the brokenhearted And binds up their wounds [healing their pain and comforting their sorrow].

Jeremiah 1:5 (AMP):

Before I formed you in the womb I knew you [and approved of you]...

Ephesians 1:6 (NKJV):

To the praise of the glory of His grace, by which He made us accepted in the Beloved.

Hebrews 13:5-6 (NKJV):

5 ...For He Himself has said, "I will never leave you nor forsake you." 6 So we may boldly say: "The LORD is my helper; I will not fear. What can man do to me?"

Have you ever been rejected by someone close to you? How do Jesus' words of love bring healing to your heart? Take time today to talk to Him about what He says about you.

_____

_____

_____

_____

_____

_____

_____

_____

_____

_____

_____

_____

_____

_____

_____

_____

_____

_____

_____

_____

_____

_____

_____

Jesus, You are the healer of my heart. You are
the lover of my soul. Your love is the only thing
that truly makes me whole. Thank You for reminding
me that I am not rejected because I am fully
accepted and approved by You!

– Your beloved Bride

Day 20
I Will Lead and Guide You

Good morning, My love,

When you have decisions you need to make, remember My promise to guide you through each day. Don't believe the lie that you can't hear My voice because that's not true. You are My beloved bride, and I call you by name, and I lead you. Don't rely on your own opinion without consulting Me. There are many choices that you consider each day. Rely on Me to guide you, and I will lead you in every decision you need to make.

I am your Husband, your Kinsman-Redeemer. I will bless you with a future of success. There's no need to worry, My Bride; receive My love and enter into My rest. I am the one who teaches you how to succeed and leads you in the way you should go. Yes, I will bless you with a future filled with hope.

Be intimate with Me, My love, and I will lead you step by step with everything you need. So, turn your thoughts toward Me and ask Me to guide you, and I will cause your thoughts to be agreeable to My will, and your plans will be established and succeed.

– Your Bridegroom, Jesus

Song of Songs 5:11 *(TPT)*:

The way he leads me is divine. His leadership—so pure and dignified as he wears his crown of gold...

John 10:3 *(TPT)*:

...The sheep recognize the voice of the true Shepherd, for he calls his own by name and leads them out, for they belong to him.

Proverbs 3:5-6 *(TPT)*:

5 Trust in the Lord completely, and do not rely on your own opinions. With all your heart rely on him to guide you, and he will lead you in every decision you make. 6 Become intimate with him in whatever you do, and he will lead you wherever you go.

Jeremiah 29:11 *(CEV)*:

I will bless you with a future filled with hope—a future of success..."

Isaiah 48:17 *(TPT)*:

This is what Yahweh, your Kinsman-Redeemer, the Holy One of Israel says: "I am Yahweh, your God. I am the One who teaches you how to succeed and who leads you step by step in the way you should go.

Proverbs 16:3 *(AMPC)*:

Roll your works upon the Lord [commit and trust them wholly to Him; He will cause your thoughts to become agreeable to His will, and] so shall your plans be established and succeed.

Have you ever believed the lie that you can't hear God's voice or been concerned about decisions you need to make? Jesus' words of love always bring peace to our hearts. Take time to write down what ministered to your heart from today's devotional.

_____

_____

_____

_____

_____

_____

_____

_____

_____

_____

_____

_____

_____

_____

_____

_____

_____

_____

_____

_____

_____

Jesus, Thank You for reminding me that I hear Your voice. Lead and guide me in every decision I need to make. Your promise to lead me step by step brings such peace to my heart. Thank You for causing my thoughts to be agreeable to Your will so that my plans are established and succeed. You bless me with a future filled with success because You love me.

– Your beloved Bride

Day 21
I Will Not Fail You

Good morning, My love,

You live in a world where your circumstances constantly change. One day brings good news and another a challenge. When that is your focus, your emotions will be unstable, up and down with every changing circumstance. There is only one thing in your life that will never change: My promise to you!

I've given you both My promise and My oath, two things you can completely count on. You can trust Me, My love, for I will never lie to you! Despite any circumstance to the contrary, what I say is true! So you can run to me with confidence and be encouraged with mighty strength to hold fast to your true identity in Me! For my promise is a strong and trustworthy anchor for your soul!

For I have said, "I will not in any way fail you nor give you up nor leave you without support. [I will] not, [I will] not, [I will] not in any degree leave you helpless nor forsake nor let [you] down (relax My hold on you)! [Assuredly not!]" – Hebrews 13:5 (AMPC)

Don't be distracted by the voices of this world. Let my voice be the anchor of your soul. Fix your eyes on Me, for I am the author and finisher of your faith, and you will be fearless and confident! Yes, My love, your heart will be at rest when you remember what I've promised.

– Your Bridegroom, Jesus

Song of Songs 5:15 *(TPT)*:

He's steadfast in all he does. His ways are the ways of righteousness, based on truth and holiness. None can rival him, but all will be amazed by him.

Hebrews 12:2 *(NASB, brackets added)*:

Fixing our eyes on Jesus, the author and perfecter of [our] faith.

Hebrews 6:17-20 *(NCV)*:

17 God wanted to prove that his promise was true to those who would get what he promised. And he wanted them to understand clearly that his purposes never change, so he made an oath. 18 These two things cannot change: God cannot lie when he makes a promise, and he cannot lie when he makes an oath. These things encourage us who came to God for safety. They give us strength to hold on to the hope we have been given. 19 We have this hope as an anchor for the soul, sure and strong. It enters behind the curtain in the Most Holy Place in heaven, 20 where Jesus has gone ahead of us and for us...

Psalm 112:6 (TPT):

Their circumstances will never shake them and others will never forget their example.

Psalm 112:6-8 *(NLT)*:

6 ...Those who are righteous will be long remembered. 7 They do not fear bad news; they confidently trust the LORD to care for them. 8 They are confident and fearless and can face their foes triumphantly.

Jesus wants to convince your heart that you can trust Him in every circumstance. Write down what ministered to your heart from today's devotion that persuaded your heart of this truth.

_____

_____

_____

_____

_____

_____

_____

_____

_____

_____

_____

_____

_____

_____

_____

_____

_____

_____

_____

_____

_____

_____

Jesus, when the circumstances around me
change from day to day, Your promises are the
anchor of my soul. I can be fearless and confident
because I know You will not fail me. You will
take care of me because You love me!

– Your beloved Bride

Day 22
You Lack Nothing

Good morning, My love,

I know there are times you feel like you lack in some way, but the truth is, because you are one with Me, you lack nothing! Yes, My love, your completeness is found in Me. You are completely filled with the fullness of who I am! You are more than enough. You are powerful and wise. Everything I am and everything I have is yours, for you are My beloved bride. You are capable, intelligent and qualified!

Don't believe the lie that you lack in some way because that will keep you from experiencing what I say. You are My garden of delight and I have come to live in you. You fully have Me, and I fully have you. You have My ability, My strength, and My wisdom in you to accomplish whatever is in your heart to do. Let Me tell you one more time: you lack nothing, My beautiful bride! You have My abundant supply. If you ever feel as though you lack in some way, remember who you are! You are one with Me, and you are fully sufficient in My sufficiency!

– Your Bridegroom, Jesus

Song of Songs 6:2-3 (TPT):

The Shulamite Bride ² *My lover has gone down into his garden of delight, the place where his spices grow, to feast with those pure in heart. I know we shall find him there.* ³ *He is within me—I am his garden of delight. I have him fully and now he fully has me!*

Proverbs 31:10 (TPT):

The Radiant Bride *Who could ever find a wife like this one—she is a woman of strength and mighty valor! She's full of wealth and wisdom. The price paid for her was greater than many jewels.*

Philippians 4:13 (AMPC):

I have strength for all things in Christ Who empowers me [I am ready for anything and equal to anything through Him Who infuses inner strength into me; I am self-sufficient in Christ's sufficiency].

Colossians 2:10 (TPT):

And our own completeness is now found in him. We are completely filled with God as Christ's fullness overflows within us. He is the Head of every kingdom and authority in the universe!

Psalm 23:1 (NIV):

The LORD is my shepherd, I lack nothing.

Have you ever felt inadequate or felt like you lacked in some way? What truth about you did Jesus minister to your heart in today's devotional?

_____

_____

_____

_____

_____

_____

_____

_____

_____

_____

_____

_____

_____

_____

_____

_____

_____

_____

_____

_____

_____

Jesus, I lack nothing because I am complete in You. Thank You for reminding me that I am more than enough and I can do all things through You who strengthens me. I am one with You and You are my sufficiency.

– Your beloved Bride

Day 23

You Are Lovely, Even In Your Weakness

Good morning, My love,

When I look at you, magnificent beauty is what I see. Even in your weakness, you are so lovely to Me. When I see you in your beauty, I see a radiant city, where we dwell as one. You are so pleasing to me. You are My greatest delight. My darling, you have captured My heart. It's true! Even the angels of heaven stand in awe of you!

Even when you feel weak in faith, it will never change the way I see you. I understand how you feel, for I have felt all the same emotions that you do. I was tempted with fear, doubt, discouragement, and disappointment, too; but I conquered them all for you! So come freely and boldly to My throne of grace with unreserved speech. Let it all out, My love, and share your deepest emotions with Me.

When you feel weak in faith, I will smother you with mercy's kiss and strengthen you with My grace. I love you too much to leave you there. You won't stay there long. For when you feel your weakest, My love will make you strong!

— Your Bridegroom, Jesus

Song of Songs 6:4 *(TPT)*:

The Bridegroom-King O My beloved, you are striking—lovely even in your weakness! When I see you in your beauty I see a radiant city where we will dwell as one. More pleasing than any pleasure, more delightful than any delight, you have ravished My heart, stealing away my strength to resist you. Even hosts of angels stand in awe of you.

Hebrews 4:15-16 *(TPT)*:

15 He understands humanity, for as a Man, our magnificent King-Priest was tempted in every way just as we are, and conquered sin. 16 So now we come freely and boldly to where love is enthroned, to receive mercy's kiss and discover the grace we urgently need to strengthen us in our time of weakness.

Philippians 2:13 *(AMPC)*:

[Not in your own strength] for it is God Who is all the while effectually at work in you [energizing and creating in you the power and desire], both to will and to work for His good pleasure and satisfaction and delight.

2 Corinthians 12:9 *(NLT)*:

..."My grace is all you need. My power works best in weakness." So now I am glad to boast about my weaknesses, so that the power of Christ can work through me.

Have you ever felt weak in faith? How does it make your heart feel to know that Jesus sees you as lovely, even in your weakness? What did Jesus say in today's devotion that particularly ministered to your heart?

_____

_____

_____

_____

_____

_____

_____

_____

_____

_____

_____

_____

_____

_____

_____

_____

_____

_____

_____

Jesus, oh, how You love me! You see me lovely,
even in my weakness. You never change the way You
see me. When I feel weak, I will come boldly to Your
throne of grace to receive mercy's kiss and receive
the grace I urgently need to strengthen me
in my time of weakness.

– Your beloved Bride

Day 24
I Make Your Dreams Come True

Good morning, My love,

It delights my heart to make your dreams come true, for I have placed dreams and desires within you! Within your heart, there are places you want to travel, creative ideas to be developed, and dreams yet to be experienced. You can do whatever is in your heart to do, for I am always with you. We are on an adventure together – you and Me. I came so that you might enjoy life more abundantly!

My beloved bride, there is only one thing I want you to do: simply let Me love you! Let My love define who you are and become the very source of your life. My extravagant love will pour into you until all your fears and doubts are swallowed up in My perfect love. You will be filled to overflowing with the fullness of My life in you.

Never doubt My mighty power to work in you to accomplish all of this. Yes, I will bring to pass the secret desires of your heart, your most unbelievable dreams, and exceed your wildest imagination! So, dream big, My love, for nothing is impossible if you'll only believe!

– Your Bridegroom, Jesus

Proverbs 21:21 *(TPT)*:

The lovers of God who chase after righteousness will find all their dreams come true: an abundant life drenched with favor and a fountain that overflows with satisfaction.

Ephesians 3:17-20 (TPT):

17 Then, by constantly using your faith, the life of Christ will be released deep inside you, and the resting place of his love will become the very source and root of your life. 18-19 Then you will be empowered to discover what every holy one experiences—the great magnitude of the astonishing love of Christ in all its dimensions. How deeply intimate and far-reaching is his love! How enduring and inclusive it is! Endless love beyond measurement that transcends our understanding—this extravagant love pours into you until you are filled to overflowing with the fullness of God! 20 Never doubt God's mighty power to work in you and accomplish all this. He will achieve infinitely more than your greatest request, your most unbelievable dream, and exceed your wildest imagination! He will outdo them all, for his miraculous power constantly energizes you.

Mark 9:23 *(NKJV)*:

...All things are possible to him who believes.

Take some time today to talk to Jesus about His goodness in your life. What dreams in your heart have you already experienced? What dreams have you not yet experienced? What did Jesus say in today's devotion that encouraged your heart to dream big?

_____

_____

_____

_____

_____

_____

_____

_____

_____

_____

_____

_____

_____

_____

_____

_____

_____

_____

Jesus, You have placed dreams and desires in my heart, and I know that You will bring them to pass. You are able to achieve more than my greatest request, my most unbelievable dreams, and exceed my wildest imagination according to Your power that is at work in me. You make my dreams come true!

– Your beloved Bride

Day 25

You Are My Victorious Bride!

Good morning, My love,

I've brought you to My banqueting table, and My banner over you is love. When you face a difficult situation, I'll revive and refresh your heart with My sweet promises. My left hand cradles your head, bringing peace to your troubled mind. My right hand holds you close so you can rest, secure in My unfailing love.

"Don't be afraid for I am with you. Don't be discouraged... I will strengthen you and help you. I will hold you up with my victorious right hand" (Isaiah 41:10 NLT).

I've told you these things so that you'll have perfect peace and confidence in Me. So, look from My perspective at every trial life brings. Don't believe that I don't love you or that I've failed you when you face troubles in life, for that is a lie. Nothing can separate you from My love. Despite the challenges that life brings, you have overwhelming victory; for I Am your conquering King and you are one with Me!

Look at you, My bride, arising from the difficulty to a brand-new life. Shining with My glory, you're astonishing to behold! You stand in victory above every trial. Safe and secure in My love, you declare My victory. Oh, My love, what joy you bring to Me. These circumstances are temporary. We're going to the other side, and you'll share our testimony with all the other brides!

– Your Bridegroom, Jesus

Song of Songs 2:4-6 (TPT):

4 Suddenly, he transported me into his house of wine—[I see his unfurled banner of victory covering me] with his unrelenting love divine. 5 Revive me with your [goblet of wine. Refresh me again with Your sweet promises!]... 6 His left hand cradles my head while his right hand holds me close. I'm at rest in this love.

Song of Songs 7:7-8 (TPT):

7 You stand in victory above the rest, stately and secure as you share with me your vineyard of love. 8 Now I decree, I will ascend and arise. I will take hold of you with my power, possessing every part of my fruitful bride. Your love I will drink as wine, and your words will be mine.

John 16:33 (AMPC):

I have told you these things, so that in Me you may have [perfect] peace and confidence. In the world you have tribulation and trials and distress and frustration; but be of good cheer [take courage; be confident, certain, undaunted]! For I have overcome the world. [I have deprived it of power to harm you and have conquered it for you.]

Romans 8:35, 37 (NLT):

35 Can anything ever separate us from Christ's love? Does it mean he no longer loves us if we have trouble or calamity, or are persecuted, or hungry, or destitute, or in danger, or threatened with death?

37 No, despite all these things, overwhelming victory is ours through Christ, who loved us.

Take a moment to think about the truth that Jesus spoke to your heart today. How did your heart respond to Jesus' words of love to you? What did He reveal about your identity as His bride?

_____
_____
_____
_____
_____
_____
_____
_____
_____
_____
_____
_____
_____
_____
_____
_____
_____
_____
_____
_____
_____
_____

Jesus, no matter what negative circumstance I face in this world, You already won the victory. You have deprived it of all power to harm me and conquered it for me. You are my conquering King, and I am your victorious bride, and we are going to the other side!

– Your beloved Bride

Day 26
You Are Royalty

Good morning, My love,

I want to remind you today that you are royalty! I paid a great price for you! I redeemed you from the dominion of darkness and brought you into My kingdom as my royal bride. Live in union and communion with Me, My love, and I will establish your heart in your righteous identity. Yes, your heart will truly be free!

My perfect love will cast out all your fears, and you'll no longer live in shame when you remember who you are, and take ownership of your new name. You are Mrs. I AM, the royal bride of the King of kings. You know how much I love you, and you have put your trust in Me! The thought of oppression will be far from you, and joy and peace will be the fruit of your life, when you live as My royal bride.

- Free from lies!
- Free from shame!
- Free from fear!
- Free to Reign!

Now we will go together and tell the world of My love and grace. We will tell them the Good News that they are loved, forgiven, and accepted! This is the abundant life that I came to give you. I gave My life so we could always be together! Reign as one with Me, now and forever.

– Your Bridegroom, Jesus

Song of Songs 7:1-3 *(TPT)*:

1 How beautiful on the mountains are the sandaled feet of this one bringing such good news. You are truly royalty! The way you walk so gracefully in my ways displays such dignity. You are truly the poetry of God—his very handiwork. 2-3 Out of your innermost being is flowing the fullness of my Spirit—never failing to satisfy. Within your womb there is a birthing of harvest wheat; they are the sons and daughters nurtured by the purity you impart. How gracious you have become!

Isaiah 54:4-5 *(NLT)*:

4 Fear not; you will no longer live in shame. Don't be afraid; there is no more disgrace for you... 5 For your Creator will be your husband; the LORD of Heaven's Armies is his name! He is your Redeemer, the Holy One of Israel, the God of all the earth.

Isaiah 54:14 *(NASB)*:

In righteousness you will be established; You will be far from oppression, for you will not fear; And from terror, for it will not come near you.

1 John 4:18 *(NLT)*:

Such love has no fear, because perfect love expels all fear. If we are afraid, it is for fear of punishment, and this shows that we have not fully experienced his perfect love.

2 Corinthians 5:18-19 *(NLT)*:

18 And all of this is a gift from God, who brought us back to himself through Christ. And God has given us this task of reconciling people to him. 19 For God was in Christ, reconciling the world to himself, no longer counting people's sins against them. And he gave us this wonderful message of reconciliation.

Take a moment to think about the truth that Jesus spoke to your heart. What particularly ministered to your heart from today's devotional?

_____

_____

_____

_____

_____

_____

_____

_____

_____

_____

_____

_____

_____

_____

_____

_____

_____

_____

_____

_____

Jesus, I am Your royal bride. You set my heart free from fear and shame by giving me Your very name. I am Mrs. I Am, righteous and good because I am one with You. Now we will tell others of Your love and goodness and encourage hearts with the Good News! Thank You for being so loving and good!

– Your beloved Bride

Day 27
Let Me Change the Way You Think

Good morning, My love,

Be careful how you think, My love, for your thoughts shape your life. Negative thoughts are not your thoughts because I have given you My mind. You hold the thoughts, the feelings, and the purposes of My heart!

I gave you the gift of peace of mind and heart. It was a gift of My love. I took a crown of thorns upon My head to set you free from all mental distress. I did not give you a spirit of anxiety and fear. I gave you a sound mind – focused and clear.

So, let Me renew your thoughts and attitudes by embracing what I say about you. You are righteous and holy because you are one with Me. Let Me remind you who you are, My beloved bride! Your life stands tall as a tower, like a shining light on a hill. You recognize the enemy's lies, and protect your heart and mind. My redeeming love crowns you as royalty. Your thoughts are full of life.

Let Me remind you again of this truth that has the power to set your mind free: Negative, accusing thoughts are not your thoughts. They are the enemy's lies coming from the outside to corrupt your mind. Catch them and make them bow to My resurrection life. Embrace and own the truth about your thought life. For the truth will set you free when you declare, "I have the mind of Christ!"

Your Bridegroom, Jesus

Song of Songs 7:4-5 *(TPT)*:

4 Your life stands tall as a tower, like a shining light on a hill. Your revelation eyes are pure, like pools of refreshing—sparkling light for a multitude. Such discernment surrounds you, protecting you from the enemy's advance. 5 Redeeming love crowns you as royalty. Your thoughts are full of life, wisdom, and virtue. Even a king is held captive by your beauty.

Proverbs 4:23 *(GNT)*:

Be careful how you think; your life is shaped by your thoughts.

1 Corinthians 2:16 *(AMPC)*:

...We have the mind of Christ...and do hold the thoughts (feelings and purposes) of His heart.

John 14:27 *(NLT)*:

I am leaving you with a gift—peace of mind and heart...

2 Timothy 1:7 *(NKJV)*:

For God has not given us a spirit of fear, but of power and of love and of a sound mind.

Ephesians 4:23-24 *(NLT)*:

23 ...Let the Spirit renew your thoughts and attitudes. 24 Put on your new nature, created to be like God— truly righteous and holy.

2 Corinthians 11:3 *(TPT)*:

But now I'm afraid that just as Eve was deceived by the serpent's clever lies, your thoughts may be corrupted and you may lose your single-hearted devotion and pure love for Christ.

2 Corinthians 10:5 *(TPT)*:

...We capture, like prisoners of war, every thought and insist that it bow in obedience to the Anointed One.

Take a moment to think about the truth that Jesus spoke over you. What particular phrase or scripture ministered to you today?

_____

_____

_____

_____

_____

_____

_____

_____

_____

_____

_____

_____

_____

_____

_____

_____

_____

_____

_____

_____

Jesus, thank You for giving me the gift of peace of mind. Negative thoughts are not my thoughts because I have Your mind. I will take captive every negative, accusing thought and make it bow to Your resurrection life.

– Your beloved Bride

Day 28

You Are My Dream Come True

Good morning, My love,

I want you to know how special you are to Me. I know you more intimately than anyone. I know everything about you – your heart's deepest thoughts, feelings, and desires. I am always with you in everything you do because I live inside of you. Wherever you go, My hand will guide you and My strength will empower you. I bring light into every dark place in your soul, for My love is what makes you whole. I know you so intimately that a hair cannot fall from your head without My notice. I carry you in My arms and hold you close to My heart.

Long ago, before you were ever conceived, I knew you. I watched in utter delight as you were formed in your mother's womb. I dreamed of our life together. I planned it all out before you took your first breath. Never believe the lie that you were a mistake or that you are not important. You've been part of My plan from the beginning of time. I created you to be alive – now – at this exact moment!

You are My amazing and wonderful bride. Every single moment, I am thinking of you! I cherish you constantly in My every thought. I want you to understand just how special you are. There is no one in all the world who is just like you. You are My dream come true!

– Your Bridegroom, Jesus

Song of Songs 7:10 (TPT):

Now I know that I am filled with my beloved and all his desires are fulfilled in me.

Psalm 139:1-18 (TPT):

1 Lord, you know everything there is to know about me. 2 You perceive every movement of my heart and soul, and you understand my every thought before it even enters my mind. 3-4 You are so intimately aware of me, Lord. You read my heart like an open book and you know all the words I'm about to speak before I even start a sentence! You know every step I will take before my journey even begins. 5 You've gone into my future to prepare the way, and in kindness you follow behind me to spare me from the harm of my past. With your hand of love upon my life, you impart a blessing to me. 6 This is just too wonderful, deep, and incomprehensible! Your understanding of me brings me wonder and strength. 7 Where could I go from your Spirit? Where could I run and hide from your face? 8 If I go up to heaven, you're there! If I go down to the realm of the dead, you're there too! 9 If I fly with wings into the shining dawn, you're there! If I fly into the radiant sunset, you're there waiting! 10 Wherever I go, your hand will guide me; your strength will empower me. 11 It's impossible to disappear from you or to ask the darkness to hide me, for your presence is everywhere, bringing light into my night. 12 There is no such thing as darkness with you. The night, to you, is as bright as the day; there's no difference between the two. 13 You formed my innermost being, shaping my delicate inside and my intricate outside, and wove them all together in my mother's womb. 14 I thank you, God, for making me so mysteriously complex! Everything you do is marvelously breathtaking. It simply amazes me to think about it! How thoroughly you know me, Lord! ¹⁵ *You even formed every bone in my body when you created me in the secret place, carefully, skillfully shaping me from nothing to something.* ¹⁶ *You saw who you created me to be before I became me! Before I'd ever seen the light of day, the number of days you planned for me were already recorded in your book.* ¹⁷⁻¹⁸ *Every single moment you are thinking of me! How precious and wonderful to consider that you cherish me constantly in your every thought! O God, your desires toward me are more than the grains of sand on every shore! When I awake each morning, you're still with me.*

Take a moment to think about the truth that Jesus spoke to your heart today. Which Scriptures from Psalm 139 ministered to your heart the most? Write down your thoughts.

_____
_____
_____
_____
_____
_____
_____
_____
_____
_____
_____
_____
_____
_____
_____
_____
_____
_____
_____
_____
_____
_____

Jesus, Every single moment you are thinking of me! You cherish me constantly in Your every thought! Thank you for making me feel so special and important to You. You made me amazing and wonderful and I know that full well. I am your dream come true! I love you because you first loved me!

– Your beloved Bride

Day 29

You Are Free from Every Accusing Voice

Good morning, My love,

I want to remind you of the day I rescued you! You were trapped in the kingdom of darkness. You were living under the accusing voice of the enemy. His plan has always been to destroy your life with guilt and condemnation. He whispered into your soul, "You're not good enough! You're a failure! There's something wrong with you!" He used your mistakes against you, and deceived you into believing you were defined by them.

But, oh, how My passionate love for you burned within Me! I would stop at nothing to rescue you. I came for you! I fought for you! I died and rose again to save you from every accusing voice of the enemy. I permanently erased all your sins. I deleted them all and they cannot be retrieved. They've lost the power to define you. I triumphed over the enemy and stripped him of all his authority to accuse you. I rescued you from the kingdom of darkness and brought you into My kingdom to be My bride.

The truth is, you are one with Me. You are holy, blameless, and without a single fault in My sight. But you must continue to believe this truth and use it against the enemy. Always remember what I did to rescue you, and you'll live free from every accusing voice. For you've been resurrected out of the death realm, never to return! Now and forever, your true identity is found in Me!

– Your Bridegroom, Jesus

Song of Songs 8:6 *(TPT)*:

Fasten me upon your heart as a seal of fire forevermore. This living, consuming flame will seal you as my prisoner of love. My passion is stronger than the chains of death and the grave, all consuming as the very flashes of fire from the burning heart of God. Place this fierce, unrelenting fire over your entire being.

Colossians 1:13-14 *(TLB)*:

13 For he has rescued us out of the darkness and gloom of Satan's kingdom and brought us into the Kingdom of his dear Son, 14 who bought our freedom with his blood and forgave us all our sins.

Colossians 1:22-23 *(NLT)*:

22 Yet now he has reconciled you to himself through the death of Christ in his physical body. As a result, he has brought you into his own presence, and you are holy and blameless as you stand before him without a single fault. 23 But you must continue to believe this truth and stand firmly in it. Don't drift away from the assurance you received when you heard the Good News...

Colossians 2: 13-16, 18 *(TPT)*:

13 This "realm of death" describes our former state, for we were held in sin's grasp. But now, we've been resurrected out of that "realm of death" never to return, for we are forever alive and forgiven of all our sins! 14 He canceled out every legal violation we had on our record and the old arrest warrant that stood to indict us. He erased it all—our sins, our stained soul— he deleted it all and they cannot be retrieved! Everything we once were in Adam has been placed onto his cross and nailed permanently there as a

public display of cancellation. ¹⁵ Then Jesus made a public spectacle of all the powers and principalities of darkness, stripping away from them every weapon and all their spiritual authority and power to accuse us. And by the power of the cross, Jesus led them around as prisoners in a procession of triumph. He was not their prisoner; they were his! ¹⁶ So why would you allow anyone to judge you...?

¹⁸ Don't let anyone disqualify you from your prize...

Take a moment to think about the truth that Jesus spoke to your heart today. How does it make you feel to know that Jesus rescued you from every accusing, condemning voice of the enemy?

_____

_____

_____

_____

_____

_____

_____

_____

_____

_____

_____

_____

_____

_____

_____

_____

_____

_____

_____

_____

Jesus, thank You for rescuing me from
every accusing voice of the enemy and bringing
Me into Your kingdom as Your beloved bride. I am
holy and blameless as I stand before You without a
single fault. I will continue to believe this truth and
stand firmly in it. Your love has set me free!

– Your beloved Bride

Day 30
I Am Your Provider

Good morning, My love,

It delights My heart to take care of you. I am your Provider and you are My beloved bride. I want to remind you to look to Me for your provision. Your job, your bank account, your business, or even another person, is not where your security is found! All those things may change from day to day, but I do not change, and I promised to provide all your needs.

I'll surround you with My favor. Yes, I'll guide you and bless you so that you'll have all that you need. I cause all grace to come to you in abundance, so that you'll have more than enough to be a blessing to others. You are abundantly blessed because you are one with Me. Everything I have is yours so you lack nothing! Remember, My love, you are Mine so you can rest in Me.

When you look to Me, and trust Me to take care of you, you'll experience My perfect peace. There is no need to worry, My love, I take care of the birds of the air, and I will take care of you; for you are so much more valuable to Me!

– Your Bridegroom, Jesus

Song of Songs 8:10-11 *(TPT)*:

The Shulamite Bride ¹⁰*...This is how he sees me—I am the one who brings him bliss, finding favor in his eyes.* ¹¹ *My bridegroom-king has a vineyard of love made from a multitude of followers. His caretakers of this vineyard have given my beloved their best.*

Philippians 4:19 *(MSG)*:

You can be sure that God will take care of everything you need, his generosity exceeding even yours in the glory that pours from Jesus.

Matthew 6:26 *(NLT)*

Look at the birds. They don't plant or harvest or store food in barns, for your heavenly Father feeds them. And aren't you far more valuable to him than they are?

2 Corinthians 9:8 *(AMPC)*:

And God is able to make all grace (every favor and earthly blessing) come to you in abundance, so that you may always and under all circumstances and whatever the need be self-sufficient [possessing enough to require no aid or support and furnished in abundance for every good work and charitable donation].

Take a moment to think upon the truth that Jesus spoke to your heart today. Talk to Him about His promises to take care of you, and rest in His love.

_____

_____

_____

_____

_____

_____

_____

_____

_____

_____

_____

_____

_____

_____

_____

_____

_____

_____

_____

_____

_____

_____

Jesus, I know You love and value me, and
You'll take care of me. I look to You as My Provider,
and I put my trust in You. I am abundantly blessed
because I am one with You! You are my good
Shepherd and I lack nothing!

– Your beloved Bride

Day 31

Get off the Treadmill and Dance with Me

Good morning, My love,

I want to share My greatest desire for you today. I wish above all things that you would prosper in every way, that you would enjoy health, and that your heart would be happy and filled with peace. There's nothing that brings Me greater joy than to see you living in the truth, receiving My love, and believing what I say about you!

But sometimes I see you striving so hard to get your "to do" list done, but at the end of the day, you're discouraged because you didn't accomplish all that you wanted to. Constantly trying to meet your own expectations or the expectations of others will only create stress in your life. My love, what are you really seeking to gain from all your striving? Is it value, approval or fulfillment? The truth is all those things are found in Me.

There's a better way to live, My love. Look to Me, and I'll create in you the desire and power to enjoy everything you do. I came that you might enjoy your life to the fullest. So get off the treadmill, My bride, and come dance with Me. It's time to have fun! It's time to live free! I want you to laugh and play and enjoy life! We will dance in the high places of the sky. Take My hand, My love, and let's dance together through each day. Forever, we will be united as one!

– Your Bridegroom, Jesus

3 John 2 *(KJV)*:

Beloved, I wish above all things that thou mayest prosper and be in health, even as thy soul prospereth.

John 10:10 *(AMPC)*:

...I came that they may have and enjoy life, and have it in abundance (to the full, till it overflows).

Matthew 11:28-30 *(MSG)*:

28-30 Are you tired? Worn out? Burned out on religion? Come to me. Get away with me and you'll recover your life. I'll show you how to take a real rest. Walk with me and work with me—watch how I do it. Learn the unforced rhythms of grace. I won't lay anything heavy or ill-fitting on you. Keep company with me and you'll learn to live freely and lightly.

Song of Songs 8:14 *(TPT)*:

The Bridegroom and the Bride in Divine Duet
Arise, my darling! Come quickly, my beloved. Come and be the graceful gazelle with me. Come be like a dancing deer with me. We will dance in the high place of the sky, yes, on the mountains of fragrant spice. Forever we shall be united as one!

Take a moment to think about the truth that Jesus spoke to your heart today. Write down what particularly spoke to your heart in today's devotional.

_____
_____
_____
_____
_____
_____
_____
_____
_____
_____
_____
_____
_____
_____
_____
_____
_____
_____
_____
_____
_____
_____
_____

Jesus, I look to You to create in me the desire and power to enjoy each day. You came that I might enjoy my life to the fullest. Your love defines my life. I want to laugh and play and dance with You throughout each day. Forever, we will be united as one.

– Your beloved Bride

Other Books by Connie Witter

Bible Studies by Connie Witter:

Because of Jesus
Living Loved, Living Free
Awake to Righteousness Volume 1
Awake to Righteousness Volume 2
The Greatest Love Story Ever Told
The Lord is My Shepherd: Psalm 23

Other Books by Connie Witter:

The Struggle is Over! You Have The Mind of Christ
Lies Religion Taught Me and the Truth That Set Me Free
Let Jesus Love the Weight Off of You!
Living Loved Living Free
P.S. God Loves You
21 Days to Discover Who You Are in Jesus
The Inside Story Teen Devotional
The Inside Story for Girls Devotional
Are You a Chicken Head? I Believe What Jesus says!
  – (Children's book)

You can purchase any of these resources at:

www.BecauseofJesus.com

We would love to hear how this book impacted your life!

To Contact the author, write:
  Connie Witter
  Because of Jesus Ministries
  PO Box 3064
  Broken Arrow, OK 74013-3064

Or Email Connie at:
  Connie@conniewitter.com

For additional copies of this book go to:
  www.conniewitter.com
  or call 918-994-6500

About the Author

Connie Witter is a speaker, author, and Bible study teacher. She is the founder of Because of Jesus Ministries which was established in 2006. Her best-selling Bible study, Because of Jesus, was published in 2002 and is the foundation of her life and ministry.

Connie has traveled throughout the United States and internationally, sharing the life-changing message of Because of Jesus. She has been the guest speaker at churches, men and women's conferences, ladies' retreats and meetings, and has also spoken into the lives of teenagers. She has also been a guest on several Christian TV and radio programs, and has had her own nationwide weekly TV program, "Because of Jesus with Connie Witter." She also has a weekly program on her YouTube ministry channel:

www.youtube.com/conniewitter

Her online Bible studies can be seen worldwide through her ministry website, www.conniewitter.com, and her social media pages. Thousands of lives have been changed through her ministry. If you are interested in having Connie come speak at your event, you can contact her at: Connie@conniewitter.com

Made in the USA
Columbia, SC
14 February 2020

87954058R00076